THE END OF THE WOODHEAD ROUTE

ELECTRIC TRAINS STOP HERE

Stephen Heginbotham

AMBERLEY

Acknowledgements

Thanks to my wife, Julie, for her support whilst compiling this my seventh book. Thanks also to Connor Stait and the team at Amberley Publishing. All photographs are credited accordingly. Every effort has been taken to establish copyright where none is shown on original photographs and I apologise for any photographs incorrectly credited.

Cover image copyright by kind permission of J. Salmon Ltd.

Dedication

To my wife, Julie (25 per cent of royalties will be donated to Cancer UK and Cornwall Air Ambulance).

First published 2020

Amberley Publishing
The Hill, Stroud
Gloucestershire, GL5 4EP

www.amberley-books.com

ISBN 978 1 4456 9042 1 (print)
ISBN 978 1 4456 9043 8 (ebook)

British Library Cataloguing in Publication Data.
A catalogue record for this book is available from the British Library.

Origination by Amberley Publishing.
Printed in the UK.

Foreword

There have been many excellent volumes written and compiled about the Woodhead Line, and this book is not about replicating any of them in any way. This book was originally compiled in 1981 by an aficionado of the route and a fountain of knowledge on the subject of signalling and electronics, namely Ian Blackburn, who is a good friend and former colleague of mine from my signalling and inspectorate days on the railway.

The book was intended to coincide with the closure of the core railway over Woodhead in 1981, but alas circumstances decreed it never hit the presses. The book lay, finished and in storage, at his home in North Wales after being carted around the UK for decades in various house/job moves, and it is only seeing publication now because it came about by a chance conversation one day. I offered to re-write it and reformat it into digital, along with the photographs and diagrams, which have all been scanned to a professional standard and cleaned and adjusted where necessary. My own publisher agreed to give it a go, and I hope you find it as interesting as I have found recomposing it; mammoth task though it was. I have added some additional material and photographs from other sources to better illustrate this long lost wonderful main line electric railway which should still have been operating today, had political dogma and of course money, had not got in the way!

Some of the images have deteriorated over the last forty years or so, but although they have been extensively cleaned, adjusted and digitally remastered, they still remain less than perfect, though I have included them for historical interest.

After twenty-seven years of virtually trouble-free electric working, closure of parts of the 1500V DC Woodhead system finally took place on 20 July 1981. So, this volume, I hope, will give a good documentation of this fascinating system in its final days, and give those people who never had the chance to see it, a good idea of what the installations and places it served looked like.

The system connected Manchester and Sheffield and the yard at Wath-on-Dearne. Originally built by the Manchester, Sheffield & Lincolnshire Railway Company, in the mid-nineteenth century, it became part of the Great Central Railway before being absorbed by the London & North Eastern Railway during the grouping of the 1920s.

The electrification, though planned in the 1920s, was not completed until 1954 after nationalisation in 1948. Following completion of the Metropolitan-Vickers locomotives, they purred up the steep gradients on the system, dragging their heavy loads in all weathers, mostly wind, mist and rain, their headlights and sparking pantographs creating an eerie sensation as they wound their way into the dimly lit, 3-mile-long Woodhead Tunnel.

The characteristics of these locomotives were way ahead of their time when they were built, and in lots of ways, they still were for those thirty or so still left in service, up to the end of the through workings in 1981.

As I compile this volume, it seems almost inconceivable to me that today in 2019 a Government department and the then British Railways Board should consider closing what ostensibly was a relatively new electric railway, especially after spending millions of pounds of public money electrifying it and boring out a completely new, 3-mile tunnel under the Pennines less than thirty years previously. The trouble with Governments and bureaucratic departments looking for savings and reasons not to do things is they have no imagination and foresight.

So, we lost a vital, fast link across the middle of England, and whilst the Woodhead closure is by no means unique in British railway terms, it has to be one of the most questionable decisions ever made, along with the loss of parts of Midland and Great Central routes, both of which would be very useful today. We also talk these days of the late lamented Somerset & Dorset from Bath to Bournemouth, but perhaps we are looking at things through rose tinted spectacles, rather than the cold light of realism and practicality. In my opinion, even the S&D, or at least some of it, was worth keeping as a cross-country route to ease overcrowding on other routes.

In this age of railway renaissance, we are spending billions of pounds of public money building new railways, such as HS2, or rebuilding railways torn up in the last sixty or so years. This regeneration of public transport is not all good though, as the private sector are not particularly interested in serving the public, unless there is profit in it, whereas I was always lead to believe that some things are provided for the benefit of serving the populous for the betterment of life, railways being one of them.

You cannot blame the private rail companies for all of the failings in today's railway, because they are, after all, in it to make money, but of course they need to provide the service the public rightly demand and deserve and at an affordable price. But on the whole, it is my opinion that rail privatisation has failed and it has just become a private monopoly, operating on a state-owned system that is massively over beurocratic, and slow to respond to modernisation, and the demands, created by the switch to rail travel.

British Railways was far from perfect, I know, I worked for them, but inspite of the bad press and image it had, the core values of service were still there, and most of today's train companies can only try to aspire to the level of trains actually turning up, late or not, that British Rail had.

The 1500V DC System – Its Rise & Fall

In 1926, following two successful electrification schemes – one on some of the Tyneside lines using 600V DC third-rail system and with overhead wires on the Newcastle Quayside Branch, and the other on the freight only lines between Shildon and Newport near Middlesbrough, using 1500V DC overhead current collection – the London & North Eastern Railway proposed electrification schemes for the Liverpool Street suburban area of London, and the Manchester to Sheffield and Wath-upon-Dearne (via Woodhead) lines.

In 1931, following the 'Weir Report' on railway electrification, the London Midland & Scottish Railway and the London & North Eastern Railway companies jointly demonstrated a scheme using electrical multiple units with 1500V DC overhead current collection on the Manchester to Altrincham line. These electric multiple units were an overhead version of the Oerlikon 630V DC third and fourth-rail sets of the London Midland & Scottish Railway's North London Line, but with the exception of locomotive Nos 6701 of 1936 (which will be described later) nothing was done to the Liverpool Street or Woodhead schemes until after the war.

The Liverpool Street to Shenfield Line electrification was completed first soon after nationalisation in 1949, the Woodhead scheme followed and was completed in 1954, both schemes using the then standard system of 1500V DC. The original 1926 plan for the Woodhead Lines had to be pruned a little due to the usual lack of finance and the continuation of electrification from Guide Bridge to Manchester Central and to Hayfield being abandoned. The rest of the scheme was retained, although in Manchester the Altrincham and Woodhead electrification schemes were never connected to each other, each occupying opposite sides of London Road Station with the former London North Western Railway platforms in between, so inter-working between the two systems never took place.

Although the Woodhead line was principally electrified for freight traffic, which in those days was extremely heavy, visions existed of electrifying the passenger expresses right along the old Great Central route to Marylebone Station in London, and to the Whitemore Yard near March in East Anglia for the many freight trains heading in that direction. These visions, however, were never to become a reality because soon after the completion of the Woodhead scheme the standard voltage for new electrification schemes was changed from 1500V DC overhead, to 25kV AC at fifty cycles per second.

This was the direct result of a controversial experiment on the former Midland Railway line between Lancaster, Morecambe and Heysham, and was applied to the Glasgow, (London Midland Region), Western lines and the Eastern Region London, Tilbury and Southend, Great Eastern and Clacton extension schemes of the early 1960s.

Although these schemes used overhead current collection throughout, parts of the Eastern and Scottish Region systems used the much lower voltage of 6250V AC because of the clearances involved.

The Shildon–Newport electrification was dismantled when that line closed in 1935 and the Tyneside and Heysham schemes followed suit in the early 1960s. The old Liverpool St scheme was converted to AC using the lower voltage of 6250, thus enabling the original catenary to be retained with the same clearances and making it compatible with the new London Tilbury and Southend, Great Eastern and Clacton extension schemes to which it joined. It was finally converted to 25kV AC in 1984, several years after the Manchester–Altrincham line which was joined to the London Midland Region Western Lines in 1971, thus allowing through working and so displacing the electric multiple units of 1930. This left the Woodhead line standing out and geographically isolated, it being the only line left with the old 1500V DC system. In the Beeching report, *The Reshaping of British Railways*, of 1964 it was chosen to survive and with the opening of the massive Tinsley Yard complex in Sheffield in 1965, to which direct access had been provided, things seemed to be looking up again for the Woodhead Line.

Henceforth the line began to deteriorate and the through services to Marylebone ceased in 1960, and the section between Hadfield and Penistone lost its passenger trains when the Manchester to Sheffield services were concentrated onto the parallel Hope Valley line in 1970. This allowed for the concentration of most of the Trans-Pennine freight over the Woodhead line. However, with tonnage of freight being carried steadily dropping the overhead catenary on some of the system began to disappear rapidly, particularly the goods lines between Gorton and Guide Bridge, and the running loops between Valehouse and Sheffield.

The yard at Tinsley was rarely worked to capacity due to the drop in freight traffic and, with the continued introduction of Merry-Go-Round coal and company Block trains, gradual closure of this vast complex, which handled up to 3,000 wagons a day in fifty sidings, took place during the 1980s and 1990s, with just a much smaller yard remaining. The adjacent depot was at one time, allocated over two hundred locomotives.

Two other setbacks for the line occurred in the late 1970s. The first was a dramatic decline in the steel industry, steel being a major source of traffic over Woodhead; and the other was when some of the coal for the giant power station at Fiddlers Ferry on Merseyside began to be delivered by sea through the docks at Birkenhead, it being cheaper that way than transporting it from the South Yorkshire and Nottingham coalfields by rail. This greatly diminished the number of trains over Woodhead, particularly the Merry-Go-Rounds, and many of the other trains formerly using the

Woodhead line began to be sent via alternative Trans-Pennine routes leaving the Woodhead line vastly underused.

Electrification of the system was completed in five stages between 1952 and 1965. The first stage took in the Worsborough Branch from Wath to Dunford Bridge in 1952. The second and third stages were from Dunford Bridge to Manchester with associated branches, and from Penistone to Sheffield, respectively, in 1954, and Sheffield to Rotherwood in 1955 and into Tinsley Yard when it was opened in 1965. An Electrical Control Room was provided at Penistone for the whole system, with supply stations at regular intervals.

The tunnels included on the system were, Woodhead (3 miles 60 yds) and Thurgoland (312 yds) on the Manchester to Rotherwood Yard line, and Oxspring (558 yds), Silkstone No. 1 (286 yds) and Silkstone No. 2 (74 yds) on the Wath line. The original twin Woodhead bores of 1845 and 1852 were in an extremely poor condition and altogether not suitable for electrification, so a completely new concrete-lined tunnel was built alongside the old ones. It took six years to build and was opened on 3 June 1954, being the third longest in Great Britain, with locomotive No. 26020 (now preserved) hauling the first train through. As there were no exhaust vents in the tunnel, the movement of diesel trains through it was strictly governed, with only one an hour being permitted. It is interesting to note that the Manchester to Harwich Boat Train was diesel hauled through the tunnel until transferred to the Hope Valley Line, along with all other passenger trains in 1970, as were the Newcastle to Cardiff Freightliner trains in 1980 and 1981. The tunnel was lit with dimmed bulbs twenty four hours a day, and a control switch in Woodhead signal box was operated if staff were working in the tunnel, thus making the bulbs normal brightness. This also alerted train drivers to the presence of staff working in the tunnel. For a while in 1976, the tunnel was continually lit with strip lighting, but this was subsequently removed. The tunnel at Thurgoland was originally one double track bore, but clearances were not sufficient for the electrification of both tracks so one track was removed from the old bore and a new bore for the Down line was build alongside.

By the 1970s, the main lines between Manchester and Rotherwood largely consisted of concrete sleepers and continuously welded rail, which allowed a maximum permitted speed of 60 mph, but the Hadfield to Dunford Bridge section was reduced to 40 mph in the mid-seventies. The remaining system used conventional wooden sleepers and jointed track with subsequent lower speeds.

Except for the goods lines at Guide Bridge East Junction and Penistone, and some of the goods line signals between Sheffield Victoria No. 4 signal box and Orgreave Colliery, all running lines between Manchester and Tinsley Yard and beyond Rotherwood were fitted with colour-light signals. A mixture of two, three and four aspect stop signals were provided between Manchester and Handsworth near Darnall, and two or three aspect distant signals were provided where signal boxes were not sufficiently close together to have their starting and distant aspects respectively on the same signal head. Searchlight type signals were provided at Orgreave Colliery and Rotherwood (the main line signals being on the Fireman's side) between the two centre main lines in both directions, which caused some confusion to the unwary of the running directions. Reddish Depot, Ashton Moss, Dinting Tri-angle, Glossop Branch, and the Wath lines were all provided with a large assortment of semaphore and colour light signals including some original Great Central lower quadrant examples.

The Absolute Block system was used, except for the London Road to Ashburys West, Hyde Junction to Godley Junction, Sheffield Victoria No. 4 to Tinsley Yard via Woodburn Junction, and Attercliffe Junction (on the Shepcote Lane box area) to Darnall West section, which were worked by Track Circuit Block. 'Permissive' working was authorized on some of the goods lines and in some of the station areas. The signal boxes at London Road, Hadfield, Woodhead, Dunford West, Sheffield Victoria No. 3, Rotherwood, those in Tinsley Yard, and Worsborough Dale were all built from 1950 onwards, the others being typically Great Central.

Under the directions of Sir Sam Fay of the Great Central Railway, electro-pneumatic control handle frames were fitted in signal boxes between Manchester and Newton on the main line, also on the Wath line in Elsecar Junction, and the two Wath Yard signal boxes. Entrance/exit push button panels were installed in the new London Road and in five Tinsley signal boxes, the remaining signal boxes being equipped with either Great Central or British Railways Standard or other types of mechanical lever frames. The frames in the Sheffield Victoria boxes were supplemented with switches to operate the signals and points in the vicinity of the closed boxes at Neepsend, Victoria 1 and 2, and Nunnery Junction.

Traffic on the line in the 1970s, compared to when it was first electrified, was light. In those early days of electrification, it was more or less a case of fitting passenger trains in-between the freight trains. Merry-Go-Round coal trains dominated the scene towards the end of the seventies. Various trains also ran via Woodhead carrying steel, flyash, chemicals, and assorted wagonloads. The Broughton Lane tanker trains to the British Oxygen Company at Widnes were a familiar site on the line, as were parcels, freightliner, and passenger trains diverted from other Trans-Pennine routes.

The only sections left with regular passenger trains after the through services ceased were Manchester to Hadfield, and Penistone to Woodhouse. The Manchester to Glossop/Hadfield section was served by the electric multiple units built in 1948 and the Hope Valley and Marple Rose Hill DMUs, as far as Hyde Junction; and the Penistone to Woodhouse section was served by the Huddersfield to Sheffield and Sheffield to Retford trains, the former reversing at Nunnery Junction to gain the only remaining operational station in Sheffield on the former Midland main line.

This is the view from the main hump tower at Tinsley Yard and shows Tinsley Main and Secondary Yards, with hundreds of wagons (predominantly coal wagons), and the vast array of sidings stretching into the distance. It emphasises the vast amount of land then owned by the state-owned railway and which, like many other parts of the network, has been sold off like the family silver. (I. Blackburn)

A Class 31 diesel looks on as wagons rattle over the main hump at Tinsley Yard in September 1980. Note the piping between the rails supplying oil for the wagon retarders. The Reception Sidings lie in the cutting beyond the bridge. (I. Blackburn)

This photograph was taken on the diminutive Woodhead Station looking towards the old and new Woodhead tunnels. (I. Blackburn)

Motive Power

The year 1936 saw an entirely new design of electric locomotive. L.N.E.R. Bo-Bo No. 6701 was jointly designed by Sir Nigel Gresley and Mr H. W. H. Richards and was completed at Doncaster Works in 1940/41. However, with nowhere to run it remained in store until 1947 when it was renumbered 6000 and shipped to Holland. There it was nicknamed 'Tommy', being put to work on passenger trains and on freight up to 1700 tons.

Whilst in Holland some modifications were carried out to the train heating boiler and an additional air compressor fitted. After running some half million kilometres it was returned to England in 1952. The nickname 'Tommy' was adopted officially, nameplates were fitted, and it was then renumbered 26000 and put to work on the newly electrified Manchester to Sheffield and Wath lines, where it worked continuously until withdrawn in 1970 and scrapped in 1972.

Fifty-seven EM1 locomotives were constructed following the prototype, the only difference being cab windows and door. Train heating equipment was provided in Nos 26050–57 and was added to Nos 26020 and 26046–49 in 1955. All of the EM1 type were fitted with Metropolitan-Vickers electrical equipment and were constructed at Gorton Works between 1950 and 1953. A few of them were used as shunters at Ilford Shed on the Liverpool Street to Shenfield line whilst awaiting completion of the Manchester to Sheffield and Wath lines.

Another twenty-four (Nos 26058–81) EM1 locomotives were ordered but cancelled. One locomotive, No. 26020, was specially prepared for exhibition at the 1951 Festival of Britain and it is preserved in lined black livery as part of the National Collection.

The EM1 class were designed for 65 mph running and had the heaviest axle-weight on the then British Railways, although they weighed a mere 89 tons with 1868 bhp. They had a route availability of eight. There was a commonly held belief that they contained left over armour from WW1. Certainly, anything that collided with them usually came off worse, including the massive Class 45 and 46 diesels.

In the engine room of these locomotives were two large traction motor blowers; one at each end. The high-tension electrical cupboard was locked with the pantograph, so preventing entry whilst the locomotive was 'on line'. The passenger locomotives that had train heating fitted, had a 250-gallon capacity boiler rated at 360kW, whilst the freight locos had a cast iron weight fitted in order to keep balance.

The reason some of the EM1 freight locomotives were fitted with train heating equipment, was that there were insufficient locomotives to cope with the passenger train demand. This was due to there being only seven of the larger EM2 Co-Co locomotives being built of the original order for twenty-seven. The residue of the order was cancelled due to financial reasons.

The traction motors were governed by an electro-pneumatic contactor and resistance, similar to (in principle) that found in simple model railway controllers. The resistance was cooled naturally by air flow between the body floor and the roof. The motors could be placed all in 'series' or both in 'parallel' with the traction motors on each bogie being in 'series'. A weight transfer switch was also provided. This weakened the field in the leading motor of each bogie, thus compensating for the bogie tilt when starting.

Up to eight different braking systems were provided, those being: train vacuum, train air, loco straight air, automatic air, Deadman device, regenerative, rheostatic, and handbrake. The regenerative system used the traction motors resistance when not under load and at speeds above 16 mph, which turned them into generators whilst still acting as a brake to slow the train down, and returned power to the overhead, though it was restricted to avoid tripping the circuit breakers in the supply stations. In 1959 the rheostatic system was fitted for use between 20 and 4 mph and on Nos 26046–57.

Also, between 1959 and 1961 the same EM1 locos were named following a Greek mythological theme. The named locos were; Nos 26046–26057 and these were painted in Brunswick Green lined livery like the EM2s.

All the EM1 locos were allocated to Reddish Depot and in the early 1970s were renumbered as Class 76, though retaining their original number order (001–057). However, at this time the named ones had their names removed. Between 1966 and 1969 twenty-one of the freight locomotives were fitted for multiple working, having jumpers fitted and dual braking. To assist in communicating with each locomotive driver when banking engines were employed on heavy trains, a system of telephones were installed called 'clearcall', which used the overhead line. To avoid tripping the circuit breakers due to excessive power being drawn, especially on the Worsborough Incline, drivers would co-operate with each other when operating over the steep sections. The locomotives fitted for multiple working were; Nos 76006–76016 and 76021–76030.

Nine further EM1 locos were later converted for multiple working, and at the same time had their vacuum brakes removed. Those still running in 1979 were; Nos 76031/2/4/5/7/8. At the same time the following EM1s were withdrawn and either stored or scrapped: Nos 26000, 76002/4/5/17/19/20/31/35/38/39/42/43/45/52/55/56/57. This left forty still in service by 1980.

In 1953/54 a larger version appeared from Gorton Works, this being classified EM2 on Co-Co bogies with a higher gearing ratio for passenger work. Numbered 27000–06, there was to have been twenty-seven (Nos 27000–26), but with the 25kV system being demonstrated the decision to cancel the next twenty was taken, so there was only ever seven built. They were stabled at Reddish Depot and fitted with regenerative braking, having a top speed of 90 mph, though 60 mph was the system maximum. They were painted Brunswick Green from their original black livery, and at least one was painted in 'Electric Blue'. They were all named from 1959 onwards. Again, this followed a Greek Mythology theme and gave them a suitable air of individuality. Weighing 102 tons they had 2760 bhp, which was far too powerful for the passenger work for which they were designed. They were withdrawn early and stored at Bury with a view to being sold abroad, and indeed were eventually sold to Holland, where all except one were used for a further eighteen years. No. 27005 was used as a source of spares.

In 1954 eight three-car electric multiple units were introduced for the Manchester to Hadfield and Glossop services. Built by the Birmingham Railway Carriage & Wagon Company (BRCW), they were almost identical to the Liverpool St to Shenfield sets. They spent their entire life on this route never straying, except for overhaul and briefly for testing on Manchester to Sheffield in 1969 prior to those services being transferred to the Hope Valley route. Set No. 8 scraped its sides whilst traversing Thurgoland Tunnel during the test and this ended any possibility of using them anywhere else. They gave thirty years of service and when withdrawn one set was kept for preservation but has since been scrapped. The line was converted to 25kV AC in 1984 and has since had ex Glasgow Class 303s and more recently Class 323 EMUs operating the route.

Guide Bridge was a storage location for locomotives pending withdrawal and for those that had already been withdrawn. Here we see No. 76024 on an undisclosed date in the summer of 1981 where it was to remain until 1983. (J. Griffiths)

Here is No. 76006 in company with No. 76014 also at Guide Bridge in the summer of 1981. No. 14 had a story to tell, being unique amongst the Class EM1 fleet. See later photo elsewhere in the book. (J. Griffiths)

Also seen stored at Guide Bridge in the summer of 1981 is No. 76025. It was stored there until towed to Reddish Depot in February 1983, thence to Tinsley Yard and subsequently to Booths of Rotherham for cutting up in March. (J. Griffiths)

Stored here at Reddish Depot is No. 76041, which had lain unused from April 1980 to February 1983, when it was then towed to Booths for cutting up in March. (J. Griffiths)

Another of the EM1s in store at Guide Bridge sometime between 1981 and 1983. No. 76046 was formerly named *Archimedes* and numbered E26046. It was the first of the final twelve constructed and to carry names, which were given at various dates from 1959 to 1961. (J. Griffiths)

Both Nos 76009 and 76011 seen in this picture appear to be still in service when seen here at Wath Depot, but were withdrawn on 20 July 1981. They were subsequently stored at Reddish and Guide Bridge before being towed away for scrapping like most of their sisters, both being cut by July 1983. (J. Griffiths)

Passing Torside en route to Yorkshire on 23 June 1981 is No. 76054 formerly known by the name *Pluto*, which it received in 1961 at Gorton Works. It spent varying periods in storage at Reddish and Guide Bridge between 1977 and 1983, until briefly stored again at Reddish before the final journey to Booths in April 1983. (J. Griffiths)

Another of the class is seen here in storage at Guide Bridge *c.* 1981. No. 76012, like many of its sisters, was withdrawn on 20 July 1981 and stored for nearly two years pending disposal or being sold abroad. With no buyers, the majority were towed away to scrap yards or cut up on site. (J. Griffiths)

A line up of several Class EM1 locomotives are seen stored at Guide Bridge, destined to never run in service again. The date is sometime after July 1981, and nothing was done with any of them until about nineteen months later when a concerted effort to dispose of all the stored locos for scrap was made. They were taken to Reddish Depot on 28 February 1983 and left for Tinsley Yard ten days later, making a final journey in company with many others five days later. Most were completely cut up by 4 April 1983. (J. Griffiths)

Wath Depot is host to Nos 76006 and 76024 on 12 May 1981. Both had a little over two months of useful work left to complete, before they were stored at Reddish and Guide Bridge for a couple of years pending a one-way journey to meet the scrap man. Like its sister No. 76014, this one jointly worked the last scheduled train over Woodhead. (J. Griffiths)

As E26014 (No. 76014) this EM1 locomotive had been the subject of an experiment way back in August 1967 when it was towed to the GEC works at Witton, Birmingham, for conversion into an AC locomotive. The experiment was deemed unsuccessful and no others were similarly treated. It was subsequently converted back to DC. It was one of the pair that worked the very last scheduled train, 6M62, over the Woodhead route on the closure day, 18 July 1981. The other loco that trip was No. 76006. (J. Griffiths)

A superb view of EM1 electric locomotive No. 76035 cab and driving controls. Built as (E)26018 it was renumbered to 76018 and finally to No. 76035 in 1976. The original (E)26035 was withdrawn in 1970 and stored at Reddish, being cut for spares in 1971, being one of the first four withdrawn. (I. Blackburn)

EM1 locomotive No. 76031 (26044/76044) seen here at an unknown location, and on an unknown date, but obviously still in service. Stored from June 1980 at Reddish, it was restored to service in the September and not withdrawn again until July 1981 and stored at Guide Bridge until February 1983, when it was moved back to Reddish the following month and subsequently towed across to Tinsley Yard. Dragged over to Coopers at Sheffield it resided intact for months before being cut up in February 1984. (I. Blackburn)

EM1 No. 76003 rounds the curve where the Rockingham Colliery line joins the electric line at Wombwell with a Dewsnap to Wath train of coal empties in April 1980. No. 76003 was previously numbered 76036 and before that No. 26036. Stored (U) four months later, it was subsequently withdrawn in July 1981 and after being stored was cut up by Vic Berry of Leicester in May 1983. (I. Blackburn)

EM2 E27000 *Electra* standing at Platform 1 in Manchester Piccadilly *c.* 1960. Built in December 1953 and named *Electra* in August 1959, she was withdrawn in September 1968 and sold to Netherlands State Railways one year later, receiving the number 1502. Subsequently repatriated, she is now preserved on the Midland Railway at Butterley. (R. Cornfoot)

A study in profiles. EMU Class 506 Motor Brake and Driving Trailers set Nos 6 and 1, respectively, wait at the bufferstops in Manchester Piccadilly on 7 May 1980. (I. Blackburn)

With just days left in service here we see EM1 76040 with a train in an unidentified location on 23 June 1981. It was withdrawn just twenty-seven days later and stored at Reddish Depot until April 1983. Towed to Frank Berry's at Leicester on 15 April 1983. (J. Griffiths)

The System in Detail Before the 1981 Closure

Manchester Piccadilly to Guide Bridge

Travelling in the Up direction towards London Marylebone Station, the Woodhead line starts in Manchester Piccadilly Station, formerly known as London Road prior to the rebuilding in 1960, which coincided with the electrification of the lines from Crewe under the 25kV AC system. The lines into Platforms 1 to 4 were wired with overhead at 1500V DC for the Woodhead route, and for use of trains to Hope Valley and Marple Rose Hill, and the truncated former route to Macclesfield Central.

Platforms 5 to 12 are wired under the 25kV AC system for trains to Stockport, Stoke-on-Trent, Crewe, and London, and other non-electrified routes beyond Stockport. Platforms 13 and 14 are for the original 1500V DC line to Altrincham, which were converted to 25kV AC in 1971 for through working.

Setting out from the Northern most tracks, London Road (Piccadilly) power signal box and Mayfield Goods Depot are passed on the right. Travelling on a viaduct, the 1500V DC share the same overhead gantries as the 25kV AC lines which run alongside, but of course the two systems are not in any way connected. Passing over the pointwork connecting the two lines we reach Ardwick Station where the Woodhead route diverges to the left and the former LNWR route carries on towards Longsight Depot, which can just be seen. Ardwick has staggered platforms, one for the Up line with a low section at the Manchester end and an island platform for the Down line and the long Down passenger Loop, which ends here.

It is served only by the New Mills and Marple (Rose Hill) trains. Opposite the island platform is a connection into Ardwick Coal Concentration Depot, and the rows of coal wagons stretching into the distance under a veritable forest of overhead wires and catenary is a familiar sight to passengers travelling towards Stockport.

On the left a grey, forbidding viaduct brings a line in from a north-westerly direction from the ex-Lancashire & Yorkshire lines at Philips Park, on the north-east side of Manchester. This line was electrified for approximately three quarters of a mile to the site of Midland Junction signal box. This line joins the Woodhead line just beyond Ashburys signal box. A few yards on is Ashburys Station which has three platforms, one with buildings serving the Down main line, whilst an island platform with a rather ineffective looking canopy serves the Up main line and the Down goods line.

This is the first station that Hadfield trains stop at. Ashburys signal box is another hundred or so yards further on and controls the junction where the main line to Romiley and the Hope Valley turns away south-eastwards. On the north side is Ashburys Yard, with approximately fifteen roads and is the site of Gorton Sheds. Here also was the former Priory Junction signal box. The two additional lines, which started at Ashburys West, merge into the main line here, the overhead wires still being in situ over the former tracks which, though now absent, clearly show where they were lifted out of the ballast. Originally these two lines carried on right through to Hyde Junction.

Plunging into a cutting Gorton Station is passed, two of its former four platforms looking forlorn on the north side, and the signal box of Gorton Junction adorning the Manchester end of the Down main platform. This signal box controls where the two additional lines from Ashburys West merge into the main lines and the triangle to Reddish Depot and Trafford Park. 100 yards further on, the junction forming one side of the triangle to Hyde Road Junction is passed and the lines turn away southwards.

Continuing in this wide cutting, the solitary double track runs alongside the trackbeds on the north side to Fairfield Station where the line forming the third side of the Hyde Road triangle joins the main lines from the south-west, just beyond the station. Five of the original six platforms still stand but only two are now in use. Due to a projected racecourse at Fairfield Reservoir, the station once had a reputation of being the largest on the Great Central Railway, but today it is unmanned.

Further along the cutting an additional Up line turns out of the Up main line and occupies the northernmost trackbed. Passing under the Stockport to Ashton Moss line, Stockport Junction is reached. This is a three-way junction at the east end of Guide Bridge Station. The lines from the north were originally electrified to Ashton Moss North Junction, on the former Lancashire & Yorkshire line, joining the Stockport line at Crowthorne Junction and the catenary masts are still in situ. The lines from the south were never electrified and come from Stockport via Reddish South leaving the Ashton Moss line at Denton Junction.

Guide Bridge Station has four platforms all in good repair, though only two are used. The Down and Up platforms have a number of buildings which contain various railway offices, but all of the buildings on the island platform have been demolished and bus shelters have taken their place. At the Manchester end, beyond the main road overbridge, Stockport Junction signal box nestles between the main lines and the Stockport lines, whilst at the Sheffield end on the Down side stands Ashton Junction signal box. Just beyond is the locomotive depot, now just a signing-point for train crews with room for stabling twenty-five or so locomotives. A good variety of classes of locomotive can be seen here at or around Guide Bridge Station, and in the days of express trains most of them stopped at this once important station for connections and local commuting.

This is Manchester Piccadilly Station as viewed from Platform 2. The former LNER side of the station (formerly London Road), which included Platforms 1 to 4 was the domain of the Woodhead electrics as well as other services. Here we see a Cravens and a BRC&W diesel multiple units (DMU) in Platforms 1 and 2, respectively, and two Hadfield electric EMU sets in Platforms 3 and 4. As a youngster, I used to stand and watch the EM1 and EM2 locomotives here and wonder at their fascinating names. (I. Blackburn)

An undated photo *c.* 1980 showing journeys start. This is Platform 1 at Manchester Piccadilly Station looking out towards Ardwick, with the 1500V DC Woodhead lines on the left and the 25kV AC lines to the right on the viaduct. (I. Blackburn)

A cravens DMU on a Manchester to Marple Rose Hill working on 7 May 1980, seen here at Ardwick Station. The points the train is traversing form the connection into Ardwick Yard and are worked by the Ground Frame to the right of the leading cab. (I. Blackburn)

Ardwick Station with Hadfield Set No. 8 about to work a Hadfield to Manchester Piccadilly train on the summer of 1980. Due to a mishap which happened during a test run through Thurgoland Tunnel, the centre coach of this set was repaired and ended up slightly wider than the rest! (I. Blackburn)

Ardwick Station, looking east. A DMU can be seen disappearing towards Ashburys, whilst a Class 08 shunts wagons in the adjacent yard. (I. Blackburn)

A solitary passenger is seen alighting from EMU 506 set number M59606M (set 6) at Fairfield Station from Hadfield in April 1980. Note the disused platforms and trackbeds of the former Goods Lines in the background. (I. Blackburn)

Hadfield EMU Set No. 8 clatters into Ashburys Station on a Manchester to Hadfield service in May 1980. (I. Blackburn)

An empty and de-electrified East Yard basks in the midday sunshine at Ashburys in May 1980. (I. Blackburn)

Hadfield EMU set No. 8 rumbles off towards Gorton on a sunny morning in April 1980. (I. Blackburn)

Ashburys Station looking East with the signal box in the foreground and the yard beyond. Just past the signal box, the line to Romiley can be seen turning away to the right with the end of electrification just out of the picture. (I. Blackburn)

Gorton Station looking towards Manchester with the signal box on the Down platform, whilst on the right are the derelict platforms which served the two additional lines to Guide Bridge. Note that the catenary wires are still in situ when this photograph was taken *c.* 1981. (I. Blackburn)

Gorton Station looking towards Guide Bridge, with the lines to the right turning away towards Reddish Depot, whilst on the left the two trackbeds continue towards Fairfield. (I. Blackburn)

Fairfield Station showing lines from Reddish on the right and the redundant trackbeds on the left. (I. Blackburn)

On 22 July 1982 a couple of Class 40s are resident on Reddish Depot. No. 40126 was built in December 1960 at English Electric Vulcan Works and was withdrawn from Carlisle Kingmoor in February 1984 and cut up at BREL Doncaster two months later. (A. Walker)

A Class 40 and a Class 25 at Reddish Depot on 22 July 1982. The electric locomotives and EMUs have finished and only a few are still stored there awaiting disposal. (A. Walker)

Class 76s shunt a DMU trailer coach at Reddish Depot in May 1980. (I. Blackburn)

An unidentified Class 40 diesel skirts the wasteland within the Ashton Moss triangle, on the south-west side, with a train of Hyfit wagons in May 1980. (I. Blackburn)

Ashton Moss South signal box faces away from the now electrified lines towards a factory wall! *C.* 1980. (I. Blackburn)

A view from Guide Bridge Station looking towards Ashton Junction in 1980. This junction was a very busy place until the Woodhead line closed, and although it is still an important junction it is, like much of today's railway, only a shadow of its former self. (I. Blackburn)

Guide Bridge East signal box, with the former Great Central lower quadrant signal serving the Down goods two line. Dewsnap Sidings can be seen beyond the road overbridge. (I. Blackburn)

Guide Bridge North signal box looks more exposed now that the lines in the yards have lost their overhead wires, in this bleak view of a railway in decline, looking towards Dukinfield *c.* 1980. (I. Blackburn)

A 'spotters' paradise! This is Guide Bridge Locomotive Sidings in May 1980 and features an impressive line-up of EM1 locomotives. The photo is undated, except for the month, but with this number of locos present it probably means the photo was taken on a Saturday. (I. Blackburn)

Guide Bridge East Junction in 1980, and some former Great Central Lower Quadrant signals are still in use amid the overhead gantries and plethora of other railway equipment. (I. Blackburn)

A view of Stockport Junction in Guide Bridge, with the Denton Junction lines to the left and the Ashton Moss lines to the right. (I. Blackburn)

Here is Ashton Bridge signal box with Guide Bridge locomotive sidings beyond. The date is *c.*1980. (I. Blackburn)

The medium wave local radio transmitters tower above Ashton Moss North signal box on a dismal day in 1980. The final gantry marks of the limit of electrification, seen on the left of the picture. (I. Blackburn)

Ashton Junction looking towards Guide Bridge North with the Permanent Way Depot in the foreground. (I. Blackburn)

End of electrification in more ways than one. This is Dukinfield devoid of the wires in Summer 1980. (I. Blackburn)

Guide Bridge to Woodhead

Continuing eastwards towards Sheffield four running lines exist, the north pair being used for freight traffic. At the east end of Guide Bridge Station, a triangle is formed between Ashton Junction, Guide Bridge North Junction and Guide Bridge East Junction. The line beyond the north junction was electrified to Dukinfield, the signal box of which had, in its final years, only one shift between the odd hours of 8 p.m. and 4 a.m. Alas, the wires have now been removed and what was once a busy parcels train yard stands decaying, along with a permanent way depot on the west side of the triangle. The line northward continues to Stalybridge, the last connection with the former Lancashire & Yorkshire (L&Y) lines before the Pennines. Locomotives were forbidden to cross the viaduct at Dukinfield, so electrification proceeded no further.

Back on the main line, two additional Down goods lines are provided between Guide Bridge East Junction and Ashton Junction as well as the four running lines. A genuine electropneumatic lower quadrant former Great Central semaphore home and distant signal exists, splitting the single additional Down goods line from Hyde Junction into two as far as Ashton Junction. Passing under a road overbridge and climbing, Dewsnap Sidings are passed on the north side. Beneath the vast expense of overhead wires stands the usual Class 08 shunting engines, the T.O.P.S. Office, shunters cabins, and a signal box. This signal box only controls the connections from the sidings to the northern pair of running lines. Beyond the brick-lined cutting on the other side of the next road overbridge is Hyde Junction. This station serves only the Woodley and Romiley lines, which slowly diverge in a south-easterly direction at this point leaving the Woodhead lines in the form of a normal double track. The surrounding scenery, which since leaving Manchester has been predominately industrial and urban, gives way to suburbia and the first sights of the foothills of the Peak District.

Newton Station is passed, and after crossing over the new M57 Motorway we reach Godley Station. Four holding sidings are situated on each side of the main lines at the Sheffield end, and the signal box stands at the end of the Up platform. Coming in from the south-west is the line from Woodley, which left the Hyde Junction to Romiley line at Apethorne Junction. The line is on the Woodley Junction signal box area coming under the wires at Brookfold. Brookfold signal box is situated at the south-west end of the disused platform of Godley Station and controls what must be one of the shortest block sections on British Rail, as it is only three or four coach lengths long. Most of the Woodhead freight traffic arrives here for a change of traction.

In the distance can be seen the new station at Hattersley, a simple island platform situated at the end of the goods loops, where Godley East signal box used to reside. This was built to serve the large new housing estate on the north side of the line, and a new interchange for Greater Manchester buses has been built outside the glass booking hall. Of course, Hattersley is synonymous with the terrible crimes surrounding the Moors Murders in the 1960s.

The line then continues through a very deep cutting, which is in fact a tunnel that was opened out during electrification. It then climbs to Broadbottom Station, which serves a more exclusive area, and then crosses over the tall Etherow Viaduct to Mottram.

Mottram No. 1 signal box disappeared in the late 1970s, so no connection from the exchange sidings further on exists from the Up line. The Down exit line, from the exchange sidings, plunges away behind a line of trees here running below (but alongside) the main lines on the south side to the exchange sidings, which are situated some half mile further on.

Mottram Yard was constructed in 1935 and was set in a massive cutting which was separated from the main lines by a strip of grass. The main hump yard is now just an expanse of wasteland, there now being only eight exchange sidings left. These are mainly used for traction changeovers when Godley and Brookfield are congested.

A halt is also provided here for staff who need to get to the yard to work trains and other duties. Although not for public use, it is served by the normal Hadfield services as well as throughout the night and at weekends by an unadvertised service between Manchester, Glossop and Hadfield.

At the Sheffield end of the yard stands Mottram No. 2 signal box. As the Great Central Head Office was situated in Manchester, all signal boxes were numbered from the Manchester end. This signal box provides connections from the exchange sidings to and from the Up and Down main lines.

Dinting Viaduct is crossed, beyond which Dinting Station lies in the shadow of the hill with Mouselow television transmitter on top. The mill town of Glossop, with the dramatic backdrop of the Peak District and Castle Hill, is now visible to the south. The single-line Glossop Branch forms a triangle to the south of Dinting Station, and a platform serving the Hadfield trains is provided on the west side of the triangle opposite which is the Dinting Railway Centre, with its steam locomotives. This has a connection on the single line to Glossop.

The main lines are provided with platforms which are kept in good condition, although they are now only used by a few rush-hour trains. The signal box stands on the Down main platform and controls the complete triangle of lines and Glossop Branch, along with the passage of trains over the enormous structure of Dinting Viaduct. At the Sheffield end of the station an Up goods line is provided to Hadfield, allowing freight trains to be turned away from Hadfield trains coming off the east side of the triangle.

Now, in the foothills of the Pennines, comes the little town of Hadfield (since made famous as the setting for Royston Vasey, the fictional town of

League of Gentlemen cult comedy series). The station here marks the end of the suburban services from Manchester. Only one of the four original platforms exist, the trains reversing on the Up line to return to Manchester via Glossop and Dinting. A modern signal box stands at the Sheffield end of the Up platform. Nearly half a mile further on past the disused goods yard on the Down side, a Down goods line from Valehouse joins the Down main line.

The scenery now changes dramatically as the hills flanking the Longdendale Valley get steeper and wilder. At the other end of the goods line, in Valehouse, a sand-drag is positioned next to the rails. This is for runaway trains coming down from Woodhead and loose coupled freight trains are forbidden from using the route in the Down direction when Valehouse signal box is switched out (closed). Should a runaway occur, the driver of the train would continually sound short blasts on the whistle/horn all the way down from Woodhead, and the Woodhead or Torside Signalman, or both, would comply with a special instruction and send the bell signal 5-5-4 to the Valehouse Signalman, who would set his points for the sand-drag.

> While the traction may have then been provided by modern electric locomotives, the track and signalling were still to a much older pattern, the signalling in particular was still stuck in the Victorian era, as in many places throughout the U.K. So, communication about trains was (and still is in some areas) made by a system called Absolute Block, which uses a series of bell codes, tapped out on Morse type instruments to describe the train or anything associated with the train, or track, or other event. When I was a young signalman in Derbyshire, my old Inspector used to say that we could train a monkey to pull the levers, you will earn your wages when it all goes wrong and you need to think quickly and on your feet. He was dead right of course!

Back to the route as it used to be. The steady uphill gradient from Manchester becomes a steep climb beyond Dinting Viaduct, being a steady 1 in 100 from Dinting to just beyond Valehouse, thence at 1 in 117 to Woodhead. The electric locomotives tackle the gradients with apparent ease, even though the maximum line speed drops from 60 mph to 40 mph at Hadfield. Indeed, it seems strange to think that trains coming downhill are providing power to take the trains uphill in the other direction thanks to regenerative braking systems, a kind of funicular railway I suppose.

Continuing from Valehouse, the track-bed of the old Up goods line to Torside, Crowden and Woodhead runs alongside the Up main on the Up side, and the last cottages alongside the A628 road on the north side of the valley can be seen. This road follows the line right along the north side of the valley to Woodhead.

As the line winds its way past the sizable Torside Reservoirs and Torside Dam, which carries the ancient Pennine Way, and with the A628 road on the far side, Torside signal box and level crossing is passed, and the Woodhead Pass looms in the distance. Trackbeds flank both the Up and Down lines as there was also a Down goods line from Woodhead and Crowden to Torside. Passing the site of Crowden Station, which used to be a traction changeover point when the EM1s were first being tested. The wild and treeless skyline now also has another dominating feature; the huge electric pylons of the National Grid.

Progressing around the curve, the climax of the line is reached, and the forbidding portals of the old and new Woodhead Tunnels comes into view along with a cluster of cottages and an electrical substation. This is a wild and desolate location, and the silence is only occasionally broken by the passage of electrically hauled trains and bleating sheep. A modern signal box stands on the Down platform, complete with central heating, though in the late 1970s it was switched out frequently due to lack of staff. The box controls a cross-over and solitary siding which has several connections in it, all with nothing stabled on them.

This is all that remains of the former Up goods lines, the trackbed of which has flanked the Up main lines from Valehouse. The A628 road sweeps up and over the hill, the lorries toiling up the steep gradient looking like toys or models against the surrounding, awe-inspiring, bleak countryside that is Woodhead.

The portals of the old single bore tunnels lie to the left, now caged up as they carry the National Grid high voltage cables through the hill linking the two sides of the Pennines electrically. Looking at them, one cannot help but understand how the old locomotive enginemen used to dread entering the dark, forbidding abyss and labouring through them. They used to have to put wet rags across their faces to stop themselves from choking on the fumes and praying that their trains did not stall inside the tunnel. The trackbeds leading to the old tunnels were severed following the removal of the bridge which used to carry the railway over a wide stream that ripples through, but a concrete catwalk has been provided for C.E.G.B. employees.

Before plunging into the tunnel, the gradient eases to 1 in 201, and after the gentle curve to the left at the west portal the concrete-lined tunnel is dead straight for nearly 3 miles. After a seemingly endless run through this drain-like structure, with the twinkling but dim light bulbs on the Down side flicking by, a faint yellow light in the distance gradually gets larger and reveals daylight. Emerging onto Eastern Region metals at Dunford Bridge we pass another small concrete station, which used to serve a nearby hamlet situated in the middle of nowhere amid this beautiful wilderness of the wild and desolate Pennines.

Hadfield EMU set No. 6 clatters away from Guide Bridge towards Dewsnap, whilst a Class 47 diesel heads a short freight down the goods line bound for the Lancashire & Yorkshire (L&Y) lines north of Manchester. In the sidings can be seen several EM1s and Diesel locos, *c.* 1980. (I. Blackburn)

The Class 08 shunter, since unofficially named 'Dewsnap', takes a break from shunting duties and stands outside Dewsnap Sidings signal box in April 1980. Built in Derby in 1959 as D3778, subsequently becoming No. 08611, she survives and is shown as with Alstom Traincare at Edge hill. (I. Blackburn)

Hyde Junction signal box sits in the gloom of a cutting. In the distance, the platforms of Hyde North Station can be seen serving the Woodley Line, whilst the Woodhead line curves around to the left towards Godley. (I. Blackburn)

This photograph depicts Hyde Junction signal box in May 1980. (I. Blackburn)

This is Newton Station and, in the distance, can be seen the high-rise flats of Hattersley and the foothills of the Pennines and Peak district. (I. Blackburn)

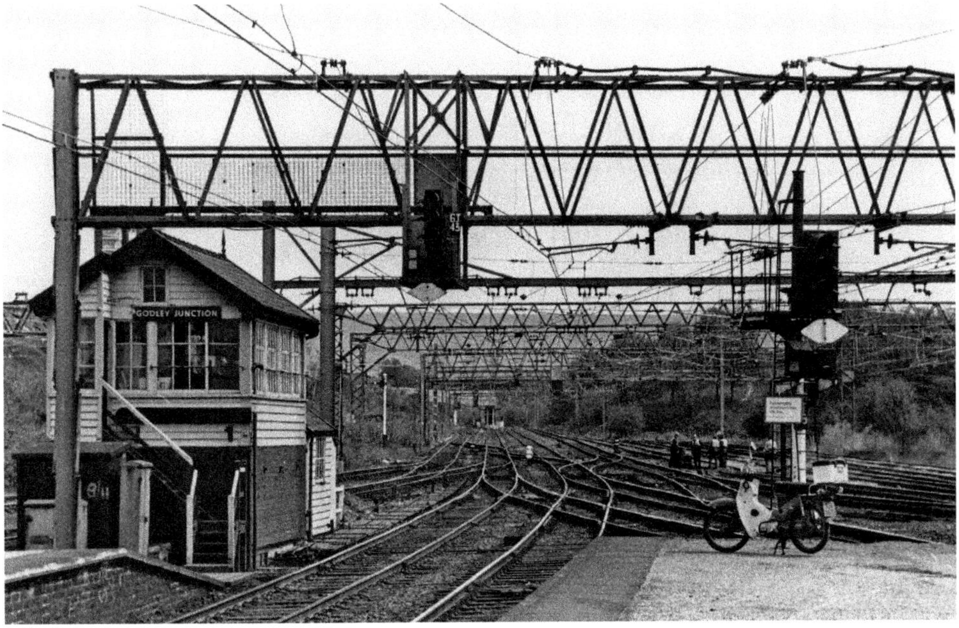

Godley Junction signal box and Holding Sidings. The new station of Hattersley, with its single island platform, can be seen in the distance. (I. Blackburn)

A train of coal wagons is in the process of changing locomotives outside Brookfold signal box in September 1980. The photo was taken adjacent to Godley Junction's home signal and illustrates just how short the block-section is. The signals on the right are Brookfold's Starter and Godley's Inner Distant. (I. Blackburn)

The end of electrification. Brookfield, looking towards Godley in September 1980. The sign in the bank reads, 'Electric Trains Stop Here'. (I. Blackburn)

A photo taken in 1989 of Godley Junction on the Woodhead route. At one time the trackbed to the left was the main route for Yorkshire Coal trains to Fiddlers Ferry Power Station. Godley Junction was the point at which electric traction gave way to diesel. Changes in coal flows and the expense of traction changeovers at both ends of the journey led inexorably to the Woodhead Routes closure in July 1981. Godley Junction had no rationale as a passenger station and was replaced by a new railway station simply named Godley but, pending formal closure proceedings, was renamed Godley East and served a handful of trains on weekdays to fulfil legal requirements. (P. Whatley)

Here we see an unidentified Class 76 at Dinting in September 1980. (I. Blackburn)

An unidentified Class 76 loco accelerates through Dinting Station having just crossed Dinting Viaduct and is bound for Wath, October 1980. (I. Blackburn)

A pair of unidentified Class 76 locos amble through Dinting Station towards Woodhead with a block train of flyash wagons in May 1980. (I. Blackburn)

Coming out of the mist in September 1980 is No. 76014 as it runs towards Hadfield with a shorter than normal freight train. (I. Blackburn)

The new Hadfield Station signal box stands at the Sheffield end of the station. Opposite the razed goods yard, the lines disappear towards Valehouse and Woodhead, *c.* 1980. (I. Blackburn)

Hadfield EMU set No. 8 disgorges its load of commuters onto the remaining platform at Hadfield before returning to Manchester via Glossop one summer evening in August 1980. Classified as 506, there were only eight three-car sets built when introduced in 1954. (I. Blackburn)

EM1 No. 76004 rumbles through Hadfield with a train of scrap metal for Dewsnap in September 1980. No. 76004 had a somewhat chequered life, in that when it was withdrawn early it was stored at Reddish from March to May 1968. Subsequently reinstated, it was then stored at Reddish again in the following November but returned to work again shortly afterwards. It was withdrawn again in February 1977 but noted working on 27 March. It was reinstated in August 1977 but stored immediately afterwards. It was withdrawn again in June 1978 and locked up inside Reddish Depot (unsold) until towed to Ashburys Yard in May 1983, and subsequently towed to CF Booths in Rotherham on 1 December 1983. It suffered a hot axle-box en route so was detached into Earles Sidings in Hope, Derbyshire, where she stayed whilst repairs were carried out. It departed again on 13 January 1984, arriving at Booths on the same day and cut up in February. (I. Blackburn)

A pair of Class 76 locomotives working the single line sections after the abandonment of the Up and Up loop lines following a derailment at Dinting. (J. Griffiths)

Standing well back from the track is Valehouse signal box, which is situated above one of the reservoirs. The 'Sand Drag' in the Down loop starts just beyond the pointwork seen here opposite the box. (I. Blackburn)

An eastbound train of Merry-Go-Round wagons with the usual double-headed Class 76 purring away, rumbles past Torside signal box in May 1980. (I. Blackburn)

Rumbling past Torside Crossing in May 1980 is EM1s Nos 76011 and 76016 (on one pantograph only) with a Wath to Fiddlers Ferry Merry-Go-Round train. No. 76011 was withdrawn in July 1981. Like many of its class it was moved between Guide Bridge, Reddish and Tinsley before making its final journey to CF Booth of Rotherham in March 1983, being cut up in the June. A similar fate was had by its sister loco No. 76016, but it arrived at Booths on 31 March after suffering a hot axle-box en route, like many of its sisters did on their final journeys. She was cut up within two weeks. (I. Blackburn)

Above: The isolated hamlet of Dunford Bridge (with its station) stands at the eastern end of the Woodhead Tunnels. Set in this forbidding landscape is the old course of both the railway, in the centre, and the old trackbed and tunnels, which are on the extreme right of the photo. Photo *c.* 1980. (I. Blackburn)

Right: The view looking along Longdendale from above the new tunnel and with Woodhead Station below and Torside Reservoirs in the Distance. (I. Blackburn)

A view looking west, of the Down platform and signal box at Woodhead in 1980. (I. Blackburn)

Dunford Bridge to Sheffield Victoria

The modern signal box at Dunford West stands on the Up platform, and it is interesting to note that prior to 1969 both Dunford West and Woodhead signal boxes were equipped with King Levers, which, when pulled to reverse, released a subsidiary lever frame at the Manchester end of the signal boxes, whilst at the same time switching out of circuit the Absolute Block signalling instruments and switching in Electric-Token-Block instruments. This permitted single line working without a Pilotman to be introduced up through the tunnel at the pull of a lever. Forward thinking indeed!

Dunford West signal box still bears its maroon nameplates. This is due to the fact that before the 1960s the line came under the jurisdiction of the London Midland Region management as far as the site of Bullhouse, further along towards Penistone. An additional goods line goes around the back of the signal box and Up platform towards Dunford East some 1½ miles further on, but this is now crippled for through use because the connections there have since been removed. Connected to the Down loop are several sidings which are only used for putting off defective wagons. Originally there were six signal boxes here and on the Up side is a piece of wasteland where the lines from the old tunnels and goods yard were.

With the National Grid transmission line running alongside not far away to the north, the line descends past Dunford East signal box, the sites of the former

Hazlehead Bridge Station and Bullhouse, Thurlestone Crossing signal box, and Penistone Goods signal box to Penistone Station. Just beyond is the single line from Huddersfield, which joins the electrified line after crossing the massive viaduct just short of the station. This viaduct is a prominent landmark in this pleasant South Yorkshire town. Between Penistone Goods signal box (which like its counterpart at Dunford East, spends almost one hundred percent of its time without a signalman) and Penistone Station, is an additional Up goods line, whilst on the Down side is a long siding and goods shed.

The line turns south-eastwards as it passes through Penistone Station, which before 1970 was served by the expresses. The scenery, which at Dunford Bridge was that of a wild and treeless moorland, has gradually changed to become the beautiful rolling hills of South Yorkshire. The buildings on Penistone Station were demolished in the late 1970s with the exception of those on the short Down platform on the Huddersfield line. The Electrical Control Centre for the entire 1500V DC electrical supply system is situated here, and on the east side of the station are the sidings in which the maintenance trains are stabled.

Huddersfield Junction signal box stands on the Down side at the junction with the Huddersfield line. As well as controlling this junction, this signal box, which is an enormous structure on stilts, also controls the junction to the Wath lines a few yards further on. These run alongside the main lines to Barnsley Junction just around the corner. The signal box there is also another enormous structure but has nothing like the importance that it once had. Thirteen electrified exchange sidings are connected to the Wath lines and are used for stabling Merry-Go-Round wagons that are used on the trains from the colliery at Dodworth on the unelectrified Barnsley line beyond West Silkstone. It is here that the electrified lines to Wath turn away eastwards, with the sidings following on the far side, before crossing a tall viaduct to plunge into the twin bores of the Oxspring tunnels.

The electrified lines to Sheffield and Rotherwood continue south-eastwards where rolling green fields abound. Blackmoor Crossing signal box is passed on the Down side. Although in working order, it is also without a signalman for almost a hundred percent of the time. Continuing down what is now the Don Valley, the line passes through the short twin bores of Thurgoland Tunnel, and with more severe curves as the valley steepens it descends towards Sheffield. The closed station of Wortley is passed, its buildings now being privately occupied, and its signal box obliterated.

The valley becomes ever more wooded as Sheffield approaches. Deepcar is passed on the Down side with its sidings and the short branch to the Fox's Steel Mill coming in from the north-west. The old station still exists and, like Wortley, its buildings are also now privately occupied. Goods loops were provided to Wharncliffe Wood, where the signal box has been reduced to a shell, but only part of the Down loop exists as a headshunt for the Fox's Branch. Further along, and still in the woods, is Oughty Bridge. The signal box here is tucked away amongst the trees on the Up side and the station, which is also closed, still stands. A small coal yard and branch to the nearby Dixon's Paper Mill are on the Down side.

Coming out of the woods the scenery changes to suburbia and industry as Wadsley Bridge is passed. The station and signal box are all intact and, due to the station being used for the football specials serving the nearby Sheffield Wednesday Football Ground, modern mercury lighting is provided. To the north on the Down side, and to the south on the Up side, are the sidings and loops for the local coal traffic and for the stabling of coaching stock for the football specials. At the south end of the north sidings, a former Great Central lower quadrant goods signal is still in existence.

Continuing southwards the sites of Parkwood Sidings, Neepsend, and Sheffield No. 1 and No. 2 signal boxes are passed and Victoria Station is reached. Neepsend is also the location of a well-known coach builder named after the Sheffield district it resides in. Neepsend Coachworks is predominately a bus and coach body makers and a subsidiary of East Lancashire Coach Builders of Blackburn.

Sadly, the station was neglected after closure, but remained in a reasonable condition until the demolition men moved in during mid-1980. Originally it had seven platforms and two goods lines on the Up side. A bi-directional line was separated from the goods lines by a glass partition. This line was served by an island platform which served the Up main line on the other side. In between the Up and Down main lines was a middle line. Two bay platforms at each of the north and south ends were set into the Down main platform. The only track that now exists is the goods lines and the Up and Down main lines. The Great Victoria Hotel, a huge grey brick building, stands at the front of the station on the Down side, hiding the decay behind it.

Signal boxes stand at each end of the station; No. 3 at the north end, and No. 4 at the south end. No. 3 controls the junction where the main and goods lines converge and out towards Neepsend, while No. 4 controls the Down goods, Down and Up main lines, and junction in and around Nunnery. The line, a wide overgrown verge separating the goods lines from the main lines, slowly curves to the left after leaving Victoria. The Midland main line is crossed, and on the Down side a double track emerges from Broad Street Tunnel on the Midland line and climbs to join the Great Central line at Nunnery. The old signal box here used to be a Midland Railway wooden structure situated on the Down side, working the connections to the carriage sidings which lie just beyond on the same side of the main lines. These sidings are used to store the locomotive hauled coaches from the main line trains in and out of the Midland Station.

The outlook is decidedly industrial as the line approaches Woodburn Junction, where the two lines from Tinsley Yard turn away to the east. Here the order of running lines changes Up goods, Down goods, Up main and Down main, to Up main, Down main and Down goods. Apart from where the Up goods line starts at Darnall, after the line from Tinsley Yard rejoins the main lines, they continue in this manner to beyond the extent of the electrification at Rotherwood with the Up goods line running on the up side of the Up main line.

The eastern portal of the 3-mile-long new Woodhead tunnel. This imposing structure pierced its path through the Pennines, the spine of England, and was a major engineering achievement that served for less than thirty years. A complete waste of both public money and a very useful resource. (I. Blackburn)

The remote, desolate and bleak location that Dunford West signal box and Dunford Bridge Station are situated in is seen here *c*.1980. (I. Blackburn)

This photograph depicts Thurlestone signal box, which controlled a small level crossing between Dunford and Penistone, *c.* May 1980. (I. Blackburn)

On a wet and windy day at Penistone in April 1980, EM1 loco No. 76001 waits for the 'road' to Wath. As No. 26001, this loco was the first production locomotive and was built in October 1950. Withdrawn in November 1980, it was moved to Tinsley Yard on 13 April 1983 and transferred to C.F. Booth at Rotherham the same day and was cut up within days. (I. Blackburn)

This is a picture depicting Huddersfield Junction signal box and shows maintenance from the local Signal and Telegraph Department (S&T) in May 1980. (I. Blackburn)

This is the lofty Barnsley Junction signal box as seen in September 1980. (I. Blackburn)

Pulling away from Barnsley Junction in September 1980 are Nos 76010 and 76013 with a Merry-Go-Round train from Dodworth to Fiddlers Ferry. Both locos lasted ten more months in service and were cut up in the summer of 1983 in Rotherham. (I. Blackburn)

A pair of Class 76s rumble past Barnsley Junction with a Dewsnap to Tinsley freight working on 18 September 1980. (I. Blackburn)

EM1s Nos 76027 and 76014 arrive at Barnsley Junction from Wath to work a Merry-Go-Round train to Godley. Taken on 2 September 1980. (I. Blackburn)

EM1 No. 76038 and another unidentified member of the class await 'the road' at Barnsley Junction with a train of hoppers. (I. Blackburn)

This is Deepcar signal box and derelict station in May 1980. The station buildings behind the signal box are now privately occupied. In the distance, to the left of the signal, the Fox's Branch to the steel mill bears to the left. (I. Blackburn)

A local coal merchant loads his lorry (Bedford TK) whilst a Class 08 shunting locomotive lies idle at Deepcar in May 1980. (I. Blackburn)

Here is a photograph depicting Wadsley Bridge and signal box and seen here looking south with the goods shed in the distance. (I. Blackburn)

Oughty Bridge looking south showing the derelict station buildings and platforms *c.* 1980. (I. Blackburn)

This is a picture of Oughty Bridge signal box which nestles amongst the trees on a humid afternoon in August 1980. The line in the foreground bearing down to the left, leads to the nearby Dixons Paper Mill. (I. Blackburn)

Wadsley Bridge looking north. The station here is used for football specials for the nearby Sheffield Wednesday Football Ground. The signal which can be seen in the yard is a former Great Central relic. (I. Blackburn)

A view of Sheffield Victoria signal box taken *c.* 1980, and showing signs of neglect. (I. Blackburn)

Sheffield Victoria Station lies surrounded by the inner city and its industry, in this district view in 1980. (I. Blackburn)

A picture taken inside Sheffield Victoria Station shortly after the demolition men moved in during May 1980. A complete waste of a large city centre station which could have served the people of Sheffield by providing a fast and clean link across the Pennines to Manchester and beyond. (I. Blackburn)

Sheffield Victoria No. 4 signal box had only a few levers left in it by this time, with the majority of its area being controlled by a panel installed in the 1970s. (I. Blackburn)

Another view of Sheffield Victoria Station South End taken in April 1980. Seen here after its demise this once busy location would see countless daily heavy freight trains pass through, and many local and long-distance passenger services providing a vital commuter and cross-country link. What a useful station and route this would be now. (I. Blackburn)

Sheffield Victoria to Woodhouse

After passing the Darnall DMU sheds on the Down side the lines from the Woodburn Junction to Tinsley line at Attercliffe Junction come in from the east and join the main lines opposite Darnall West signal box. This signal box is on the Down side and controls all of the connections to the DMU sheds, as well as the junction to Tinsley. A few yards further on stands Darnall Station, now without a canopy. This island platform's remaining brick buildings stand empty and heavily vandalised.

The line now passes through a cutting and under a heavy iron road overbridge before passing under a concrete overbridge, which carries one of the main feeder roads from the M1 Motorway to Sheffield city centre at the start of Handsworth. The line emerges from the cutting and enters coal mining country. On the Down side is an area which has been returned to farming, while on the Up side slag heaps are being landscaped. Beyond here the floodlighting towers of Tinsley Yard and the M1 Motorway can be seen some half a mile distant.

Orgreave Colliery is approximately a mile further on. The signal box is situated in the cutting here on the Down side, and opposite are the unelectrified sidings for the stabling of wagons for the adjacent pit. Meanwhile, further back are nineteen sidings on the same side of the line, also used for the stabling of wagons for the pit.

Emerging from the short cutting the connections to the north end of Rotherwood Exchange Sidings are passed over. These are operated by the signalman at Orgreave Colliery signal box and the running lines are flanked by five exchange sidings on the Up side and four on the Down side. The electric locomotives are stabled at the Orgreave Colliery end of the Down sidings. At the southern end of these sidings, on the Up side, stands the modern signal box of Rotherwood. This marks the limit of electric traction. Electrification continues for another couple of hundred yards for both Up lines, stopping just short of Woodhouse Station as the railway passes through a spur of Sheffield's suburbia. This station is unstaffed with its two platforms flanked by the goods lines on each side of the station. The buildings are still standing, and modern mercury lighting is provided.

Beyond Woodhouse Station the electrification lines enter a wide cutting with a number of sidings on the Down side to Woodhouse Junction. Extensive Permanent Way sidings flank the old Great Central main line to Beighton Station Junction, where access to the Midland main line is provided via Barrow Hill to Chesterfield. The old Great Central main line then continues in the form of a single line to Arkwright Colliery, while what is now the main line curves away eastwards from Woodhouse Junction towards Worksop and Retford.

Two Class 08 shunting locomotives are seen here marshalling coaches in Nunnery Carriage Sidings, near Sheffield Victoria Station, in April 1980. (I. Blackburn)

Nunnery signal box was a Midland Railway structure that controlled the entrance to the Carriage Sidings at the top of the incline from Sheffield Midland Station. Here it stands (just) in a dilapidated, windowless and gutted condition, which it had been since Sheffield Victoria No. 4 signal box took over its area in May 1980. (I. Blackburn)

The lines at Sheffield Midland Station are seen here diving into the tunnel at Nunnery in this undated photo *c.*1980. Note the 'catch point'. (I. Blackburn)

A very atmospheric photograph depicting Darnell Shed, taken in 1980. (I. Blackburn)

This is Darnell Servicing Shed as seen in April 1980. (I. Blackburn)

This is the Up side of Darnell Station, showing its dereliction in this picture from May 1980. (I. Blackburn)

This is a view through the complicated array of overhead line wires and equipment as seen at Darnell west signal box *c.* summer 1980. (I. Blackburn)

Orgreave Colliery signal box and a Class 31 diesel waits to cross over from the Down main to the Up goods line in order to collect the wagons on the right of the picture, which have just been drawn out of the Coking Plant Sidings beyond the bridge, in May 1980. (I. Blackburn)

This photograph, taken one evening in May 1980, shows that Rotherwood signal box lies in a tranquil setting. (I. Blackburn)

Owing to a major derailment at Wharncliffe early in 1980, a number of Class 76 locos were stranded in Tinsley and Rotherwood. Here six of the class lie idle at Rotherwood in March 1980. (I. Blackburn)

Electrification continues over both Up lines stopping just short of Woodhouse Station, as seen here on a misty morning in May 1980. (I. Blackburn)

Gorton Junction & Fairfield to Reddish Depot

The lines from Gorton Junction and Fairfield meet 1-mile after leaving the main lines, both passing through cuttings to reach this point. After passing under a road bridge the cuttings open out where the two lines meet just short of Hyde Road Junction signal box. The line crosses the top of a high embankment and heads in a southerly direction. The signal box stands at the top of the embankment on the west side of the line and some fifty yards further on a small patch of waste ground lies to the east side of the line. This is the former site of five sidings, only one of which was electrified. With the embankment reducing in height, the line curves slightly to the left, the trees on the embankment giving the line a more suburban atmosphere.

Immediately after crossing the Ashburys to Romiley line, about three-quarters of a mile beyond the signal box, the connections to the relatively modern Reddish Depot are reached. The depot was built in 1948/9 and is separated from the main line by a grass verge. It caters for the local diesel locomotives as well as being the principle depot for all of the 1500V DC fleet. Immediately beyond the depot a road overbridge crosses the line and depot spur. Electrification of the main lines stops before this bridge. The lines carry on curving to the right before coming onto the Manchester London Road (Piccadilly) Power signal box area and becoming a single line to Trafford Park on the western side of Manchester.

A Class 40 diesel leaves Reddish Depot running light engine to Dewsnap Sidings, in May 1980. (I. Blackburn)

Awaiting their next turns of duty outside Reddish Depot, in May 1980, are Class 76s Nos 76008, 76021, 76027. Formerly they were (E)26008, (E)26021 and (E)26027, all surviving to the end of the 1500V DC system. All were cut up by Booths of Rotherham in 1983. (I. Blackburn)

An unidentified Class 40 at Reddish Depot in April 1980 in company with another classmate. (I. Blackburn)

A sad scene at Reddish Depot as we see No. 76050 dumped, minus bogies and pantographs, in April 1980. Built as (E)26038 it was withdrawn in February 1977 and was due to be towed to Crewe Works but the move was cancelled. By September 1977 it was robbed of its pantographs and in April 1978 it was grounded without its bogies. With space at a premium, in March 1983 it was put back on bogies and towed to Ashburys Yard for storage and remained there until November 1983, being then towed to Booths at Rotherham and was scrapped during February 1984. Ironic that it was one of the first withdrawals, but yet one of the last to be scrapped! (I. Blackburn)

This is a picture inside Reddish Depot and shows No. 76011 and an unidentified Class 40 on 7 May 1980. I spent many a Saturday afternoon in the early 1960s wandering around here; a truly fascinating place. (I. Blackburn)

Number 76023 (E26023) was just another of the many stored at Reddish, from July 1981. This picture, however, might imply that it was just out of service rather than withdrawn as the loco behind it has the pans up and appears to be in service. Date unknown. (J. Griffiths)

EM1 number 76003 (originally numbered E26036 then 76036) seen at Reddish and appears to be in store, which it was from 27 August 1980. Originally sent for possible overhaul to Crewe works in June 1968, it was back in store at Reddish Depot by November 1968 but returned to service shortly afterwards. (J. Griffiths)

Barnsley Junction to Wath

Leaving the main lines to Sheffield and Rotherwood at Barnsley Junction the two Wath lines swing around to the east, along with the thirteen exchange sidings, before crossing over a tall viaduct and plunging into the twin bores of the Oxspring Tunnels. Like the Sheffield line it is downhill all the way to Wath.

West Silkstone Junction is where two unelectrified lines to Dodworth Colliery and Barnsley bear to the left, whilst the two lines to Wath continue downhill. At West Silkstone there used to be a Down goods loop and on the Barnsley line, on the Down side, the old banking engine siding still exists. This siding is electrified, and in times past played host to the former L.N.E.R. Beyer-Garrett 2-8-0 + 0-8-2 locomotive. This massive engine was built in 1925 as No. 2395 and later became No. 9999 and subsequently No. 69999 under British Railways in 1948. It was the longest and most powerful steam locomotive built for use in Britain. Principally working from here to Wath, banking heavy coal trains up the steeply graded Worsborough Bank, it was later tried out on the Lickey Incline in 1948/9 and then back to the Woodhead route for a while in 1955.

The signal box, which is on the Up side before the junction, is very hard to find from the road and is reached after passing through a farmyard. All the trains are banked from Wombwell Main Junction to West Silkstone Junction, the Merry-Go-Round trains using two multiple-controlled EM1 locomotives as bankers. The site of two EM1s pulling thirty or forty loaded Merry-Go-Round wagons with another two EM1s pushing at the rear is impressive. The banking engines are often attached to the front of loose coupled trains going downhill from West Silkstone to Wombwell main to provide additional braking power. The sight of three or four locomotives heading a train towards Wath is not uncommon.

The Worsborough Branch, as this section of line is called, passes through the two short Silkstone Tunnels (286 yds and 74 yds) before heading out into the beautiful Yorkshire countryside to Wentworth. A single line branch from a nearby colliery, which was closed in the mid-1970s, comes in to join the Worsborough Branch from the south-west and the signal box, which stands on the Down side of the line, is disused and heavily vandalised. The line then crosses the M1 Motorway on a long iron bridge before passing the site of Strafford Crossing signal box and skirting the extensive suburbs of Barnsley which lie to the north. The line now begins to descend, not constantly but in a series of steps not unlike a flight of canal locks. It begins to take on the atmosphere of a Swiss rack railway due to the maximum permitted speed of only 20 mph caused by the ground being honeycombed with old mine workings.

Kendal Green Crossing is the first operational signal box on the Worsborough Branch, and is the first in a series of four level crossings all within a mile of each other. Worsborough Bridge signal box controls the next crossing, and unlike the others is provided with modern lifting barriers.

The next signal box is Glasshouse, which, unlike the other three on the Down side, is on the Up side of the line. The line then passes where the post-war box of Worsborough Dale was until the end of the 1970s.

The squat little signal box at Lewden controls the final crossing before reaching the bottom of the branch at Wombwell. It is interesting to note that all of these crossing boxes were worked by women until the end of the 1970s.

The Midland Railway Sheffield to Barnsley line crosses the Worsborough Branch on a tall viaduct as the electrified line turns south-east and becomes flanked by three loops on the Up side, and two loops and the trackbed of a third loop on the Down side. This is Wombwell, which is the base for the banking locomotives of the Worsborough Branch. As the line turns sharply eastwards again, an unelectrified double-track branch from the colliery at Rockingham comes in to join the electrified lines opposite Wombwell Main Junction signal box on the Down side of the line. The branch, however, is only a double track for approximately a mile to Dovecliffe Level Crossing, continuing as a single line beyond there to the colliery.

The line then turns almost immediately south-eastwards again, this time a bit more gently, before the unelectrified line from Barnsley, with the connection from the Midland Railway main line from Cudworth to Stairfoot Junction, joins the electrified lines from a northerly direction at Aldham Junction. The signal box here is on the Up side of the line on the final curve before Wath Yard. A rusty spur on the Up side marks the spot where the old Up line and Down main lines were and the trackbeds continue, along with the redundant overhead masts, right down to Elsecar Junction. Just a stones-throw from Aldham Junction is Mitchells Main signal box. This is a small affair controlling the level crossing here which is provided with modern lifting barriers.

The line descends for another half a mile past Darfield Main signal box where a colliery line from the adjacent pit comes in from the north-east. Several exchange sidings are situated here on the Up side of the line beyond the signal box, which is on the Down side. The overhead wires in these sidings are installed on a continental basis, as they are in most of Wath Yard. The wires are slung between two masts, instead of being on droppers slung directly from the gantries.

The line enters a shallow cutting and continues downhill with the trackbeds and all too familiar redundant gantries on the Up side. Civilisation is now becoming evident towards the south-west with houses and shops appearing on the horizon. After passing a semaphore distant signal, which has been fixed at caution, the two lines split into four where the single line (which is also unelectrified) from Elsecar Goods comes in from the west. Crossing over a level-crossing the order of the running lines becomes, Up main, Down main, Up goods and Down goods. This is Elsecar Junction. The signal box stands on the Down side, and controls the level-crossings as well as the junctions and the north end of Wath Yard, which now looms in front, its vast expanses of continental style wiring looking awesome and top heavy.

In the distance to the north-east, diesel hauled expresses can be seen crossing the flat countryside on the parallel Midland Railway main line. A double junction beyond the signal box takes the arrival and departure lines to and from the vast exchange yard, which parallels the four running lines right up to beyond the Motive Power Depot, which is on the Up side of the line some three quarters of a mile ahead. Only the Elsecar Junction end of these sidings is electrified, except for a few places further on.

Two small signal boxes, Wath Sidings 'A' and Wath Sidings 'B', work the two humps between the groups of sidings within the yard. These humps were the brainchild of Sir Sam Fay, who was the chairman of the Great Central Railway Board, and were installed when the yard was built in 1908. Electrification of the Down goods line continues only for a few yards to the rear of Elsecar Junction's home signal, and further down the same line a former Great Central lower quadrant distant signal, now fixed at caution, still survives. The Down main line is electrified to the point where the lines to the Motive Power Depot turn off on the Up side and run parallel to the four running lines.

With only the two Up lines now electrified, a grey iron road overbridge loom ahead. Connections from the motive power depot join the Up and Down main lines. Following the double crossover from the Up to Down main to the Up and Down goods, the extremity of the electrification is reached a few yards short of the bridge.

Looking ahead just beyond the bridge among the connections at the south end of the yard is the squat signal box of Moor Road Bridge, which works the Up and Down goods lines and the associated yard connections. Further in the distance is the larger signal box of Wath Central, which controls all of the other lines in the vicinity. Beyond the collieries and steaming chimneys, which are characteristic of this area, the line continues into the Yorkshire coal mining country, passing the Midland Railway's main line to Sheffield and Wakefield before being joined by the Sheffield to Doncaster lines at Wath Junction, 2 miles short of Mexborough Station.

On 18 September 1980 a Class 45 diesel roars past West Silkstone with Merry-Go-Round (MGR) hoppers from Dodworth bound for Barnsley Junction, where a pair of Class 76s will work the train forward. The line disappearing down to the right is the Wombwell Branch to Wath. (I. Blackburn)

Class 76 No. 76038 and its partner develop some wheelslip as they begin to haul a heavy train of Merry-Go-Round wagons out of Oxspring Sidings at Barnsley Junction in May 1980. (I. Blackburn)

This photograph shows the diminutive ground level Kendall Green signal box taken *c.* 1980. (I. Blackburn)

One of the 'steps' of the Worsborough Branch can be seen in this view from Kendall Green looking towards West Silkstone. On a wet day in April 1980. (I. Blackburn)

EM1 Electric loco No. 76038 was the Wombwell Banking Engine the day this photo was taken in May 1980. Here it is seen on a misty Monday morning at Worsborough Bridge, on its way to conduct a train from Barnsley junction to Wombwell and increasing that trains brakeforce in the process. No. 76038 was originally numbered 76050 and before that No. 26050 (Stentor). Withdrawn in July 1981 it was scrapped in May of 1983. (I. Blackburn)

This photograph shows (to good effect) Worsborough Bridge Crossing signal box looking up the 'steps' towards Kendall Green in 1980. (I. Blackburn)

Any high-sided vehicles, over 17 feet tall, trying to cross this crossing would certainly create a disturbance with all the (Phosphor-Bronze) bells strung across the road here at Glasshouse Crossing. (I. Blackburn)

The small Crossing Keeper's Cabin at Lewden *c.* 1980. (I. Blackburn)

Having just detached the two banking engines from the front of the train at Wombwell, No. 76014 moves away towards Wath in May 1980. The locomotive had just over a year left in service, being withdrawn in July 1981. It was towed to Booths of Rotherham and cut up in May 1983. (I. Blackburn)

This is a photograph of Wombwell Main signal box taken *c.* 1980. (I. Blackburn)

This is Aldham Junction signal box which stands on the final curve before Wath. The line to Stairfoot, Barnsley and Cudworth disappears in the foreground, whilst the electric line to Wombwell bears away to the left. The line in the immediate foreground is all that is remains of the main lines, which now end at Mitchells Main, a few yards further on. (I. Blackburn)

Old and new stand side by side at Wath Depot in May 1980. A pair of Class 76s and a Class 56. (I. Blackburn)

A pair of unidentified Class 76s make their way out of Wath Yard past Elsecar Junction signal box in May 1980. (I. Blackburn)

Here is Wath 'B' signal box and Hump. (I. Blackburn)

Shown here is the end of electrification at Moor Road Bridge just beyond the limits of Wath Yard. This photograph was taken in 1980. (I. Blackburn)

This is Moor Road Bridge and was situated at far end of Wath Yard and marked the end of the Woodhead electrification. The tracks from here onwards take the route southwards through Mexborough and Doncaster. (I. Blackburn)

Woodburn Junction & Darnell West to Tinsley Yard

The two lines from Woodburn Junction and Darnell West both descend through cuttings and around curves for about a quarter of a mile to meet at Attercliffe Junction.

Now heading in a north-easterly direction the line passes alongside the heavy steelmaking factories that are so typical of this area, while on the Down side a canal is situated alongside the line. An additional electrified loop line, which has connections to the steel works, runs along the Up side of the Up line to beyond the derelict station at Broughton Lane, about half a mile further on. The line now curves to the left here and various sidings flank the Up side of the line, whilst on the Down side, electrification is only provided for the additional Down line from Broughton Lane Junction. At this junction the two electrified lines bear round to the right, while the four unelectrified lines, the additional one of which is out of use, continue on to join the maze of freight only lines in and around Rotherham.

After about half a mile, two lines – the first one of which comes from Brightside on the Midland Railway's main line from Sheffield to Wakefield and

Leeds, and the second one of which comes back to form a triangle from the four lines which the electrified line left at Broughton Lane – meet the electrified line at Shepcote Lane Junction. This is the western entrance to Tinsley Yard. After a complicated junction, two electrified lines continue around the back of the power signal box to the north-east side of the yard and the Express Freight Yard, which has seven roads, all of which are electrified. The electrified engine line from the reception sidings, which are right at the other end of this massive complex, are just over a mile away.

Meanwhile, the main electrified arrival line, which is called the South-West Arrival and is just over a mile in length, runs around the south-western boundary of the yard along with the completely electrified secondary yard, which was under threat of closure. The electrified Express Freight Yard to Tinsley Park lies on the other side of the secondary yard, which closed in October 1980. A line turns out of this arrival line, climbing the grass embankment to enter the British Steel Corporation works at Tinsley Park, before coming back down again to rejoin the South-West Arrival line beyond the Secondary Yard Hump.

The electrified Engine Line to Tinsley Park and the Express Freight Yard emerges from under the Secondary Hump, which is situated a little further back, and climbs to reach these connections which are just short of the Breakdown Crane Sidings and Diesel Servicing Depot. The Engine Line then goes around between the Diesel Servicing Depot and Breakdown Crane Siding and the Main Yard Hump, whilst the South-West Arrival Line dives under the line which rises from the connections to the Motive Power Depot, which is situated on top of the south-west embankment flanking the reception sidings.

Coming around to the maze of tracks in the vicinity of the main hump, the South-West Arrival and Engine Return lines pass under the Wood Lane overbridge and enter the vast wide cutting in which nestles the Reception Sidings; seven lines of which are electrified. Tinsley Power signal box is set into the south-west embankment and is a line that has been the scene of several spectacular locomotive runaways, rising to the Motive Power Depot, which is situated on top of the embankment.

This cutting is the home of the rather novel Class 13 'Master and Slave' shunting locomotives, which are formed from two standard 0-6-0 diesel shunting engines, one of which has had its driving cab removed, whilst the other had a radio-telephone for communication with the hump towers, shunters and the Tinsley signalman. There is also a system of cab signalling for the hump towers fitted. Both the main and secondary humps are fitted with hydraulic wagon retarders which automatically check the speed of wagons as they run down the other side of the humps and into the various sidings.

These retarders consist of studs which protrude upwards inside the running rails, so making the flanges on the wheels of the wagons tread or press them down as they run into the sidings. If a wagon is going too fast, the force needed to depress the studs by the flanges is greater, so slowing the wagons down, while if the wagon is travelling at or below the correct speed the resistance of the studs on the flanges is minimal, so permitting the wagon to run down unhindered. In the main yard, only sidings numbered thirty-four to forty-six are electrified, access being gained from the Express Freight Yard at the Tinsley Park end, which is on the north-east side of the complex towards Shepcote Lane.

At the other end of the Reception Sidings, a large concrete bridge spans the cutting and carries the feeder road from Sheffield City Centre, which crosses the Rotherwood line at Handsworth between Darnell and Orgreave Colliery to the M1 Motorway, which has run on an elevated section along the entire length of the north-east boundary of the complex. The electrification ends just under this bridge in the engine spurs and the unelectrified lines split before being carried over the grey brick viaducts. This forms a triangle with the Chesterfield to Rotherham via Barrow Hill and Beighton Junction line at Treeton Junctions.

This is Broughton lane looking east *c.* 1980. (I. Blackburn)

Here is a view of Shepcote Lane and the entrance to Tinsley Yard taken *c.* 1980. (I. Blackburn)

An unidentified shunting loco and the 'Master & Slave' shunting locomotives in Tinsley Yard in May 1980. Master & Slave No. 13002 takes a break from duties as it stands in the deep cutting which contains the Reception Sidings. These were rebuilt from D4187 (Master) and D3697 (Slave) and was one pair of only three sets so converted. (I. Blackburn)

A Tinsley 08 shunting locomotive creeps around under the M1 Feeder Road Bridge to the end of the electrification in May 1980. (I. Blackburn)

An unidentified Class 37 diesel loco passes up the south-west arrival line at Tinsley, en route from Rotherwood to Tinsley Motive Power Depot (M.P.D.). (I. Blackburn)

EM1 locos Nos 76032 and 76034 double head a train out of the Express Freight Yard past a Permanent-Way tamping machine at Shepcote Lane in September 1980. Both were withdrawn in July 1981 and cut up in March 1983. (I. Blackburn)

Broughton Lane looking west. Wagons for scrap metal stand in the sidings for Brown Bayley beyond the bridge, *c.* 1980. (I. Blackburn)

An industrial locomotive shunts wagons of scrap outside the Brown & Bayley Steelworks between Attercliffe Junction and Broughton Lane in May 1980. (I. Blackburn)

On 2 September 1980 we see EM1s Nos 76029 and 76010 back up the Engine Line from the Reception Sidings to the Express Freight Yard at Tinsley. Note in the background a long line of brake vans which are either stored as surplus and awaiting scrap, or just stabled awaiting their next turn of duty. (I. Blackburn)

A busy scene on the south-west Arrival Line at Tinsley Yard, with Nos 76036 and 76029 and a freight from Dewsnap and in the background are wagons being shunted over the main hump. (I. Blackburn)

Class 40 No. 40101 joins up with its train at Tinsley Park on 2 September 1980. Built at Vulcan Foundry as D301 in November 1960. When this photograph was taken, she had less than two years left in service and was cut up at Crewe in November 1984. (I. Blackburn)

Woodhead Doomed

In early 1980 the British Railways Board ended a lot of rumour and speculation by proposing the complete closure of the Woodhead Route. Amid loud protests the Penistone to Sheffield passenger service was withdrawn. The only sections allowed to survive were the Manchester to Glossop and Hadfield section, and a single line from Nunnery Junction in Sheffield to the Fox's mill at Deepcar.

The demolition men moved in quickly to Sheffield Victoria Station and by the summer of 1980 any chance of a reprieve was dashed. The whole affair seems such a waste, bearing in mind that the permanent way, tunnels and signalling equipment were in reasonably good condition, although the overhead wiring needed some attention largely due to the 'maintenance holiday' in latter years. The EM1 Class 76 locomotives still gave relatively trouble-free service and had many years and miles left in them. Indeed, the Woodhead Route was the only Trans-Pennine route capable of taking 8-ft 6-in. containers without restriction. Conversion to 25000V AC was considered, it being dismissed on the grounds that the signalling was not compatible, and diesel traction was ruled out because of the lack of ventilation in the Woodhead Tunnel.

1 June 1981 was the initial date given by the British Railways Board for the total closure, along with a promise that the Woodhead Tunnel and main line trackbeds would be kept up to standard for a reasonable length of time. But with the parcels terminal at Guide Bridge already closed, and the Secondary Yard and hump at Tinsley closing in October 1980, some guards at Sheffield decided to voice their opinions on the further proposed closures by taking industrial action in the form of refusing to collect fares on 'paytrains' in the Sheffield area. This action led to a public enquiry sponsored by the National Union of Railwaymen, which held back closure until Monday 20 July 1981. However, the Godley Junction to Apethorne Junction section had been closed for some months because of a tunnel collapse between Woodley Junction and Stockport (St Georges Road), thus causing the M.G.R. trains to Fiddlers Ferry to be diverted via Guide Bridge, Denton Junction and Stockport Edgeley.

The final months of operation on the system, however, did not pass without incident. On 10 March 1981 an eastbound mixed freight train from Arpley Junction, near Warrington, to the Eastern Region, hauled by locomotives Nos 76028 and 76029, left the rails whilst passing through Dinting Station, causing immense damage and the immediate abandonment of the Up main and Up loop lines between Dinting and Hadfield. Single line working was introduced over the Down line between Dinting East Junction and Hadfield, but on 8 April a second and much more serious accident occurred on the west end crossover at Hadfield. A train of 13,100 tonne Anhydrous Ammonia tanks from Barton to Immingham, hauled by locomotive Nos 76025 and 76027, had travelled over the Down line from Dinting in the Up direction, and was regaining the Up line when five of the wagons left the rails, one of them overturning and rupturing, thus soiling its contents out onto the tracks. Because of the dangerous toxicity of the contents, nearby houses were evacuated while the mess was cleared up. Then immediately before the final week of operation, on Thursday 9 July, a massive landslip occurred near Torside. Surprisingly, the engineers arrived and by Saturday 11 July the line was cleared and reopened.

The last working to traverse up the Worsborough Branch was on Friday 17 July, when locomotives Nos 76007 and 76012, which were on banking duties that morning, cleared West Silkstone Junction at around 1.20 p.m. on their way back to Barnsley Junction to pick up a Merry-Go-Round train for Fiddlers Ferry. Work on dismantling the line between Wombwell Main and West Silkstone began immediately after closure of Lewden, Glasshouse, Worsborough Bridge, Kendal Green and West Silkstone signal boxes. The last train from Dodworth to Barnsley Junction was a train of Merry-Go-Round wagons hauled by diesel locomotive No. 45001. From now on all trains from Dodworth were to be diverted via Barnsley to Healey Mills Yard, although the track from Penistone to Dodworth was to be left in situ pending a decision on the future of the Huddersfield to Sheffield service, and whether or not to divert them around through Barnsley.

The main line between Penistone and Hadfield closed some sixteen hours after the Worsborough Branch when the west bound Harwich to Edgehill air-braked Ferry Van train, 6M65, hauled by locomotive Nos 76006 and 76014, cleared Woodhead Tunnel at approximately 5.10 a.m. on Saturday 18 July. On Monday 20 July Blackmoor Crossing, Barnsley Junction, Penistone Goods, Thurlestone, Dunford East, Dunford West, Woodhead, Torside and Valehouse were officially closed. The sidings at Godley Junction, Mottram and Oxspring were clipped out of use on the same date. Then an announcement came that the main line tracks and overhead structures (some of which near Valehouse were originally experimental ones erected in 1936) between Hadfield and Sheffield were to remain in situ for another six months, pending a decision on future railway electrification projects, although the conductor wires were removed as a safeguard against theft.

Extensive engineering works on the parallel Hope Valley line continued the attempts to bring that line up to the same standard as the Woodhead line. Standedge Tunnel on the former Lancashire & Yorkshire Huddersfield to Stalybridge line was to be modified to take the 8-ft 6-in. containers.

Woodhead's days of 1500V DC were over, the electric locomotives would no longer purr up the steep gradients dragging their heavy loads and heaving sighs of relief as they passed Dunford West signal box.

Reference Sources

Ian Allen Publishing, *Ian Allen ABC Combined Volumes 1961, 1962, 1968.*
www.brdatabase.info
www.sixbellsjunction.co.uk
Marsden, Colin J., *The Complete UK Modern Traction Locomotive Directory*, TheRailwayCentre.com, (2011).
Notes supplied by: I. Blackburn, J. Griffiths.
My own contemporaneous notes and archive records.